CORNERED

A blow by blow account of my fight with cancer

SCOTT CANCELOSI

COPPERSTATE
★PUBLISHING™

CORNERED
A blow by blow account of my fight with cancer

Edited by Rhonda Paschal

Digital cover artwork: Vintage Boxing Corner and Stool by Allen Swart
Front cover and page design by Scott Cancelosi

Printed in the United States of America

PROUDLY PRINTED
inTHE USA

First Edition

Library of Congress Control Number: 2017916114

ISBN: 978-0-692-96144-5

On the Cover: When diagnosed cancer patients often feel they are backed into a corner. You come out fighting for your life, only to find yourself time and time again against the ropes. You have to have a strategy. Learn as much as you can about your opponent; shake off the blows, stay focused, and show no mercy.

Dedication

To my wife, Anne Cancelosi, who stood by my side during my darkest hours.

I also dedicate it to all cancer survivors - may you continue to be an inspiration to others.

Acknowledgments

I would certainly be remiss if I didn't first thank the doctors and surgeons for whom without them this book would have never been written. I had listed all of the staff I had contact with at least one time that I met during my journey, but unfortunately my online blog was hacked. So here are the following names I can remember through business cards and billing statements:

Patrice Al-Shatti, Mayo Clinic
Renee Crawford, Mayo Clinic
John K. Crowe, Scottsdale Medical Imaging
Lisa Crujido, Mayo Clinic
Andy Courson, Mayo Clinic
Kelly Curtis, Mayo Clinic
John Demenkoff, Mayo Clinic
Melissa Eden, Mayo Clinic
Daniel Hurley, Valley ENT
Jan Kruse, Mayo Clinic
Noreen McCue, Mayo Clinic
Tricia Montgomery, Mayo Clinic
Paula Phillips, Mayo Clinic
Gary Robinett, D.D.S.
Sherry Tarelton, Mayo Clinic
Wanda Trimm, Mayo Clinic

And especially Michael Hinni, my head and neck surgeon; Samir Patel, my radiation oncologist; Steven Schuster, my oncologist; and my family physician who fought for the biopsy Dr. Jose (Joe) Reynoso.

Other acknowledgments
Cancer survivor and friend Don Watters.
For stopping by, and ignoring the feeding tube and scars, and BSing as guys do, Anthony "Tony" McCollum.
Additional edits by Dora Vasquez and Anne Wallace.

Foreword

Michael L. Hinni, M.D

For more than 20 years, I have devoted my professional life to the care of people diagnosed with head and neck cancer. Over this time I have observed, as have many, the rising incidence in cancer of the oropharynx.

When I started, Oropharynx Cancer represented 25 percent of the cancers I would treat and now it is over 65 percent. This rise is due to the appearance of HPV associated cancers. This rise is the bad news. The good news is that HPV cancers are much more curable than the cancers we once encountered more frequently.

Let me state clearly how moved I am, every day, with the courage of the patients and their families, when dealing with these awful malignancies. Oropharyngeal throat cancers are very difficult for all involved. Enduring the treatments are as challenging as those of perhaps any other human malignancy.

For starters, these cancers affect every basic function we hold dear, eating, breathing, talking, and even our appearance. If one finds themselves plagued with one of the more common human malignancies (Lung, Colon, Breast or Prostate), the consequences of the disease and its treatments can be hidden under a hospital sheet or under ones clothing.

Ones friends and family leave the hospital or the living room and make comments about the color, or weight of their loved one. The scars from surgery, the radiation burns, are hidden under clothing. As awful as it is, your loved one can lose a breast and yet place a prosthesis in a bra, put on her favorite gown, and go to a reception, talk to attendees, eat the cocktail shrimp, and breathe through her nose and mouth. Sadly, this is often not so for head and neck cancers.

Throat cancers, the surgery involved, the radiation effects, cannot be hidden. People see the scar, or the burn. People notice that one cannot eat shrimp or sometimes eat at all. People notice you feeding yourself with a tube. People notice you can't talk properly or that you are breathing through a hole in your neck.

This is why head and neck cancer is so devastating. This is why it is so difficult to treat, why it is so challenging for patients, their families, and their cancer care teams alike.

It has been my life's challenge, and my privilege, to help people through countless crises. Most new patients feel understandably that there is no way they could have cancer. They say, "Doctor, I can't have cancer, other people get cancer, not me, and I feel so good. There must be some mistake." And it is a life changing event. I say life changing because 90 percent of those with HPV related oropharyngeal throat cancers are eventually cured. The treatments are difficult yes, but the treatments are dramatically less harmful than in the very recent past. New surgical less invasive approaches, newer normal tissue sparing radiation protocols and less toxic chemotherapy continue to ease the burden of treating these malignancies.

The following story is one of many amazing stories of a hero who had cancer tossed onto an otherwise "normal" life. A story about a young family man who endured treatment of stage 4 cancer, survived, and took the tragedy and turned it into an amazing gift. A gift that so many of us could really use.

Michael L. Hinni, M.D.
Chair, Department of Otolaryngology - Head and Neck Surgery
Professor of Otolaryngology, Mayo Clinic College of Medicine

Photo Credit: Mayo Clinic

Table of Contents

CHAPTER 1.

Ear Ache My Eye!

New Year's Resolution

I was having a great year in 2011. I began running again as a New Year's resolution in January and for six months I was running a mile up to a mile and a half a day. Not really that far but the running was my time to decompress and release my stress.

Work had its pressures as always; many special projects and not enough time to complete them. This was and is typical of any job, and I attempted to balance work and play.

In August I began to feel a little sluggish. I stopped running and began to get irritable at even the littlest things. Something was up with my body and I knew it. My caffeine intake increased and I was very tired but pushed through the days, something I had always done.

Swimmer's Ear

On Labor Day I went swimming and thought I got some water in my left ear. Swimmer's ear, *"wonderful,"* I thought.

For weeks after the swim, I felt inner ear pressure. It wasn't until October that I went to my primary care physician Dr. Joe Reynoso to talk about the ear ache. Perhaps it was allergies? After talking with him, we both didn't think much of the ear ache as allergies are so common in our family that we both brushed the ear pain off. As for my lack of energy, he suggested, perhaps it was a sign of my age as I had just turned 45. *"Thanks Doc. Reality check."*

By late October I was sleeping a lot and started napping on the weekend. *"I am not lazy,"* I would tell myself as I attempted the *"honey do"* list: over seeding for the winter lawn and working on the home repair projects.

Singing the Tryptophan Blues

Late November rolled around, I remember Thanksgiving Day vividly. I was playing basketball with my niece and nephew. I was winded and sluggish…*"from eating too much turkey"* I thought. I got tired after five or 10 minutes of playing and had to rest. We all laughed about me being out of breath as I went inside to lick my wounds after missing easy shots. Again I wondered, *"is this because I am getting older?"*

Lymph Node Alert

It wasn't until early December that I noticed something peculiar on my neck while shaving. A small lump had surfaced under my jawbone on the left side of my neck. I didn't want to alarm anyone; I am a firm believer in not worrying about anything until I gather all of the facts. I made an appointment with Dr. Reynoso.

I've been going to him since I was a teenager and I knew my doctor well. I immediately saw the concern on his face following the examination.

He told me with a poker face that the lump could be any number of things, but a biopsy would rule out whether the lump was a cyst, some type of infection, a benign tumor or cancer. Did he just say *cancer*? He was adamant that I get a biopsy performed as quickly as possible.

I remember leaving the office with a sense of disbelief. He told me to remain positive and I knew I had to as the holidays were here, and daughter was just about to turn three. We had big plans ahead for the season.

The Big Four

The next few weeks of the holiday season were tiresome as I gathered my thoughts for my December big four - my daughter's birthday, my niece's birthday, Christmas and my wife's birthday. Oh, and don't forget about the New Year celebration.

Keeping Up Appearances

As the race toward the December holidays continued, I had to keep up a positive appearance. I hoped family wouldn't notice the lump during my daughter's birthday party in mid-December.

I was exhausted after playing the office passive-aggressive Santa with a beard as white as snow covering the lump. Did anyone notice? It took a lot out of me to show up and give a holiday performance, sweating profusely and not feeling well. Sure my doctor told me not to worry, but time was ticking away to get tests done as the lump grew larger every few days. I didn't want to have family and friends worry in the event the lump turned out to be nothing serious. My wife was the only person in whom I confided.

A Tussle with Health Insurance

Dr. Reynoso began the steps for me to get a biopsy appointment. He wanted a computerized tomography (CT) with a needle biopsy; this would ensure accuracy of the needle.

CORNERED

I was frustrated when I found out the insurance company approved an ultrasound… just an ultrasound. So I went for ultrasound imaging. Conclusion, a lump. As if we didn't already know that.

Many phone calls were made between my doctor and the insurance company as he attempted to persuade them to approve a needle biopsy for laboratory testing. I'd call him; his staff would call back; they'd call the insurance company. You get the picture.

I began to look at what the out-of-pocket cost would be to pay for a biopsy. Dr. Reynoso continued his push to see what was really going on with my body.

In the meantime, he ordered blood work. On December 24 - yes, Christmas Eve, I got blood drawn for tests.

My wife and I spent Christmas day of 2011, wearing our own poker faces as family was still not aware of my prognosis.

Breathe, Remember to Breathe

A Christmas gift arrived via a phone call from my doctor's office. An *ultrasound* with a *needle biopsy* was approved to be scheduled after Christmas.

Three weeks. It took THREE WEEKS. Seems like a long time, an eternity in my mind. My heart is saddened when I think about those vets who cannot get an appointment at the VA as their cancer grows. The mental anguish of three weeks was enough to drive me insane!

I mean, I was looking to pay out of pocket for the procedures and realized I was a lucky guy to have my doctor on my side. I was like *"wow"* the insurance company was splitting hairs – an ultrasound needle biopsy or a CT needle biopsy? It didn't matter, a biopsy needed to be done. Get it done and get it done quickly.

The only appointment I could get during the holidays for the biopsy was at a clinic in Fountain Hills, about a 25 minute drive from my house. As I drove up Shea Boulevard, I looked at the McDowell Mountains and the scenery that I've seen so many times. I remember it being a very long and lonely drive. My wife told me to call her as soon as the procedure was completed.

As the biopsy was performed, the doctor asked me several pointed questions.

"Have you been exposed to Asbestos?" he asked as he injected anesthetic into my neck to numb it.

"Hmmm. Not good," I thought.

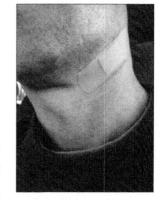

(Right) A lump on my neck is covered with a Band-Aid after a needle biopsy that was performed the week between Christmas and New Years in 2011.

Ear Ache My Eye!

"I am going to take some extra tissue samples so you don't have to come back," he explained as he wiggled a large needle in the lump, extracting tissue for testing.

"Crap, come back?" my mind answered. *"This isn't good."*

At this point my brain was like a lighting show with so many different thoughts going on it was really hard to think. Why was this lump growing on my neck? What was my body reacting to? Benign or malignant growth?

The sample would be sent to the lab over the New Year's holiday. He said when the results came in he would *personally* call me. I felt assured that he would as he placed a Band-Aid on my neck where the biopsy was performed.

Happy holidays indeed.

After the biopsy on December 29 the lump was so large I felt I could no longer hide it. I told my family about the past month, the fight for tests and the roller coaster ride of emotions.

(Left) Yes, I still acted goofy, wearing a celebratory hat on New Year's Eve despite talking about the biopsy test with my dad, Rich in December 2011.

I felt like I went through a huge battle to get the biopsy approved and completed. As the family went into New Year's, we waited for test results that wouldn't be available until after the holidays.

It was the longest New Year's weekend and it was an exhaustive month. Little did I know the battle to get a biopsy was just the beginning of the fight for my life.

CHAPTER 2.

Time Stands Still

Pathology Report

It was the morning of Jan. 2, 2012. The phone rang as I was preparing for work. Modern technology doesn't lie with caller ID and I knew who it was before I picked up the phone. He has NEVER called me personally.

"Hello is this Scott?" asked Dr. Reynoso.

I could tell by the tone of his voice his news wasn't good. I grabbed a pen and paper and went out to the back patio. My heart sank as I listened. Disbelief immediately turned into shock… time stood still.

I don't remember much about the conversation - only that it was like listening to an adult talking to Charlie Brown in a Peanuts cartoon.

"Waa, waa, waa, waa," He said. *"Squamous cell cancer. Waa, waa, waa."*

Whaaaaa….t? What is that? I have never heard of it.

My head wanted to explode when I heard the news. I tried to scribble some notes onto a piece of paper but my mind was cloudy. I had a malignant tumor; I just learned I had throat (pharynx) cancer. CANCER.

As I hung up the phone I was immediately concerned for my daughter and my wife. I turned to my wife and had to tell her I have cancer. I said it with disbelief. She cried.

A few minutes later I received another phone call. The doctor who performed the biopsy was a man of his word and personally called back with the lab results. A little calmer, I listened more clearly and learned more about squamous cell cancer.

I went to work that day and told my boss and staff about the diagnosis. Yes, I went to work.

Useless Bucket Lists

Today when I talk to anyone who is a survivor they all had the same reaction when they were told they had cancer.

"Not me, not now." Like anytime is a good time get cancer; like you are personally immune from any disease. I wasn't overweight, I didn't smoke like a chimney, and I

wasn't abusing my body. You had so much on your plate to do but haven't done what you wanted to do. Excuse after excuse along the way. I am talking about big life stuff. Spend more time with the kids or grandkids; spend more time with family and friends. But you never did it. And then there was the bucket list. They are useless to have unless you intend on checking off each item. I am not talking about mowing the lawn or going to see a movie. You never did travel to Europe or take that cruise did you? How about river rafting the Grand Canyon? Taking your kid to Disneyland? You had the bucket list but never checked off any of the items on it. Why?

CHAPTER 3.

Letting the World Know about the Fight

Quick Decisions

In early January, 2012 things fell into place and fell into place quickly.

What had lagged in slow motion in a month of trying to find out what's wrong with me, turned into me making quick 24-hour decisions.

Jan. 2, 2012

Biopsy results in.... I have cancer. They basically have to pinpoint where from. CAT and full body scan in my future. I'll be getting an oncologist number and more information on Tuesday. Don't know yet if they remove the lump on neck with surgery and chemotherapy or just do radiation with chemotherapy. Estimated time out of office, three months. Asking just for your prayers. I was actually out of the office from February to mid-June.

Fight Card Revealed

How do you notify your family and friends in 2012 that you have cancer? Social media, of course. Those who were not on Facebook I contacted through my Christmas card list with a homemade postcard.

Jan. 4, 2012

Doctor, doctor it hurts when I swallow. Then don't swallow...

My First Nasopharyngoscopy

I went to an ear, nose and throat doctor and a nasopharyngoscopy was performed. The ENT doctor squirted lidocaine in my nostrils to numb the nasal cavity before the procedure.

Then a flexible scoping device was slipped slowly up the nose down to the back of the throat to view any mass or obstruction that might be causing pain or discomfort. It would be the first of many nasopharyngoscopys to come.

Letting the World Know about the Fight

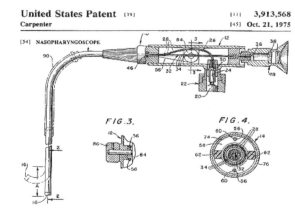

United States Patent [19]

Carpenter

[11] 3,913,568

[45] Oct. 21, 1975

[54] NASOPHARYNGOSCOPE

FIG.3.

FIG.4.

(Left) The first flexible Nasopharyngoscope was patented in 1975. Today they include flexible fiber optics with a light source attached to a monitor. (Source: U.S. Patent Office)

(Right) The photo of my throat was taken in March with a Nasopharyngoscope.

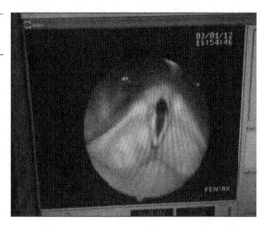

The culprit of my neck lump was clearly visible on the ENT's monitor, a tumor at the back of my throat a little bit larger than a dime. I remember one thing from this visit: How *cool* it was to actually see the tumor on the screen. Weird huh? I was impressed by the technology. I believe I had some relief that I was actually looking at the cause of my pain. I was no longer taking blind punches from a hidden cancer. I started to take medication for severe inner ear pain.

Jan. 5, 2012

Okay, I am going to say it. Life sometimes REALLY sucks. But it is better than the alternative...

My Blog Title

The title of my blog, "Don't Let the Bastard Win," says it all about my personality -abnormal. The name came from a line in a M*A*S*H episode. One of my favorite characters, Hawkeye Pierce, pounds on a patient's chest saying *"Don't let the bastard win."*

Now being served at the

Don't let the BASTARD win Cafe

Sarcasm. My mind's natural defense against cancer.

You later find out in the episode "the bastard" is death. Unfortunately, the blog was hacked a few years later and I lost my online journal. But that's something small compared to the people who read about my journey as I experienced it. The *"Bastard Café"* was posted January 13 to Facebook. I had to inject some kind of humor in a non-humorous situation. The following are some of the early blog posts.

Jan. 10, 2012

Received a phone call on Jan. 10, 2011, that my PET scan was approved and will head to Scottsdale Medical Imaging.

My positron emission tomography (PET) scan test was performed just 10 days after receiving the phone calls that I was diagnosed with cancer. A special dye with radioactive *"tracers"* was injected into my system before the scan.

Jan. 12, 2012

Pet scan done. Basically you are injected with radioactive sugar. I know, I know, sounds like a 60s band. "And now ladies and gentleman, Radioactive Sugar with special guest…"

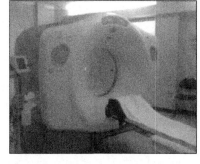

Afternoon Blog Post

Good news. Dr. Hurley's office called just before noon. "Nothing distant" (technical term: cancer metastasis, spread to other parts of the body) which means that the area is just where he says it was, back of the throat and neck. Unfortunately it did show the right lymph node with cancer.

Knowing your Opponent

In 2012, stage four squamous cell carcinoma head and neck (throat) cancer was rapidly on the rise. As of the writing of this book, it is still unclear what *causes* the mutation in the throat.

I was 45 at the time and in the age bracket of those who have been diagnosed with this type of cancer. I was told if I was exposed to HPV in my lifetime my survival rate would be higher. According to the Centers for Disease Control and Prevention, the HPV infection isn't cancer but can cause changes in the body that can lead to cancer. My doctor said HPV was more than likely the cause of my cancer but we wouldn't know until after surgery.

As the CDC states, HPV-related cancers are not common in men and most that get HPV never develop symptoms. In some men the infection never goes away. "Cancer develops very slowly and may not be diagnosed until years, or even decades, after a person initially gets infected with HPV," the CDC stated on its website in 2017.

Letting the World Know about the Fight

Fight Predictions, the Odds and Betting Line

When I was diagnosed, the online survival rate statistics were outdated. All of the doctors, from my primary care physician to the surgeon and radiologist told me not to believe the statistics - they were based on old data and people who were heavy tobacco and alcohol users.

Factors that can increase your risk of throat cancer include:

- Tobacco use, including smoking and chewing tobacco
- Excessive alcohol use
- A virus called human papillomavirus (HPV)
- A diet lacking in fruits and vegetables
- Gastroesophageal reflux disease (GERD)

Adjuvant Therapy Definitions

Chemotherapy. Chemotherapy uses drugs to kill cancer cells. Chemotherapy treats the entire body, killing cancer cells, no matter where they may be located. Adjuvant chemo-therapy isn't helpful in all situations, so talk to your doctor about whether this treatment is right for you and how much of a benefit it may provide.

Radiation therapy. Radiation therapy uses high-powered energy beams, such as X-rays, to kill cancer cells. Radiation therapy can be given internally or externally. Adjuvant radiation therapy focuses on the area around the original cancer site to reduce the risk of cancer recurring in that area.

Source: Mayo Clinic website (2016)

If I remember correctly I was told about 30,000 people a year were being diagnosed in 2012. At the time I thought I'd have a better chance of winning big cash on a lottery ticket than getting this type of cancer. Every case is different, but everyone still looks at the odds.

My fight options were pretty cut and dry: I could have radiation therapy or surgery *and* radiation therapy for my stage 4 cancer.

Radiation alone might take care of the cancer and I would be done with treatment. Then again it might not. The doctor would still have to perform surgery down the road if the radiation therapy did not produce results. I didn't know how strong my body would be after the radiation. I had a difficult decision to make. I must be candid. Your emotions will always be a stronger opponent than listening to facts and knowing the odds.

I discussed my options with family and friends. Most people said to me they would want the cancer removed by surgery if they had to make the decision.

I chose laser surgery with adjuvant therapy (radiation) treatment. I would also need a neck dissection to not only remove the lymph node that had cancer, but to remove others that had not yet surfaced. At my initial prognosis I was told I would most likely not need chemotherapy which at the time was a relief to me and my family.

CHAPTER 4.

Mental Floss – Fight Preparation

Ring-side Support, My Corner

Despite the problems with the insurance company in December, the company just started to accept insurance for the Mayo Clinic that fall.

Had my cancer shown up six months earlier I would have most likely been treated at another hospital. I actually felt blessed that the ENT and my doctor had me headed to the Mayo Clinic for treatment.

I had to find comfort in the smaller, positive aspects of my nightmare. I continued to try to find a positive in each challenge I faced but sometimes there just isn't one to find.

I had to begin mental flossing, clear my brain, and tried not to listen to the destructive clutter of punching from all directions. When I couldn't find a positive, I still tried to remain focused on the fight ahead.

I had three ring-side physicians. The first is one of the best laser head and neck surgeons in the nation, Dr. Hinni. Dr. Patel was my radiation oncologist and Dr. Schuster, my oncologist.

The positive attitude and bedside manner of these men had a huge impact on the way I was to skillfully approach the fight. They explained what was to come, the *"what ifs"* and answered all of my questions. They also answered my wife's long list of questions that I often had written on a piece of paper.

The rest of my corner staff to whom I am eternally grateful are listed in the acknowledgement section at the front of this book.

Being Prepared for a KO

Some people do not want to make decisions and think about death for whatever reason. Perhaps maybe they fear the reflection on their life and the chapters not yet written, or they think about the darkness of death instead of everlasting life.

My corner wasn't going to throw in the towel and as long as they had faith in me, I would have faith in the directions they would give me to win the fight. No one ever wants to admit they could be KO'd but life is in God's hands.

Jan. 18, 2012

Doctor says I could lose at least 25 lbs. during treatment. I normally wouldn't do this, and my heart skipped a beat just looking at it. Eat Poppa, eat. We don't need a skinny Santa. Check in at I-Hop.

I already had a living will and power of attorney completed which is called an Advanced Directive. But, I didn't have a will. Not that I really needed one as Arizona is a community property state (A.R.S. § 33-431). That basically means your spouse gets the property and belongings if you die.

You should check and see if the state you live in is a community property state. If it isn't your spouse has to go through probate to have the property transferred to them which is something that really sucks after losing a loved one. How about a trust and estate planning?

Do I sound like an attorney? I hope not. This isn't a legal advice book. I am only suggesting that you prepare for what may be to come. Contact your local bar association and talk to an attorney to create a will.

I prepared mine because I wanted to leave small things to my family and friends, certain memories that only they would appreciate. As I typed the will, I reflected on those memories. It wasn't the accumulation of *"things"* that were to be given. When I left this life I wanted to leave items that would make a loved one smile with the memory connected to it.

I completed the simple statutory will, since my um, estate (insert laughter here) is well, VERY simple. Upon completion I needed witnesses and a notary, so I simply brought the will to work. Our office commissions notaries and as two staff members signed and witnessed my signature, the will was notarized.

As strange as it sounds, when I SIGNED the will I didn't feel like I had death knocking at my door. I didn't cry. I didn't feel remorse or melancholy. Rather it was just one more thing to do before my cancer surgery and treatment.

Remember to prepare and write down special requests sometimes referred to as "My Wishes," and sign and date it.

- Do you want to be buried or cremated?
- Do you want a service at your place of worship?
- Do you want a eulogy? Who would you like to give it for you?

- Do you want a funeral or memorial service? Should there be a public viewing? Do you want family and friends to share their memories at the service? Do you want an open or closed casket? Special music?
- A grave-side service? Precession to the cemetery?

At the time I also prepared my own obituary. My wife's grandmother wrote her own and at her passing it was one less thing the family had to worry about when preparing for services. You might want to consider writing your own. How do YOU want to be remembered?

I hope anyone reading this book will make preparations for your family long before I did. It is just something in life that should be taken care of and most people do not want to do.

CHAPTER 5.

Entering the Ring - Twice

Into the Ring of Fire

The photo of a chiminea fire the evening of Feb. 5, 2012.
I was mesmerized by the flames and at the same time numb at what was about to happen to me.

As I looked into the fire, the smell of the wood brought back memories of church retreats and camping in high school. Our chiminea (outdoor fireplace) was fired up a few nights in a row a couple of days before the fight of a lifetime. Smells and sounds bring you back immediately to moments – good or bad. It's like that really bad song that came out around homecoming and sounds even worse today, but it still will bring you back to that moment with friends.

Jan. 31, 2012 ~ Final Exam

Prep Op Test Day. I didn't even study. Look out Right Said Fred, "I am too Sexy For my Gown." Can I get a gown that's fitted please? So shapeless, even with my girlish figure.

Check in at Mayo Clinic Specialty Building.

The Catholic Boy in Me

The day before my surgery I went into Blessed Sacrament's Parish office I had been in so many times since 1978.

This is the Catholic Church where I have fond memories of being part of the youth group; then sang in the teen choir and played guitar; received my Confirmation; and was married to my wife Anne.

The reason I was there this time was to receive the Sacrament of Anointing of the Sick. It wouldn't be the first time I had received this Sacrament from a priest from this church.

My junior year in high school, the same year I received my Confirmation, I was anointed with blessed oil in the hospital as I recovered from double pneumonia. At a young age I was given the reminder that life can punch you so hard in the chest, you cannot breathe. I was given an early life lesson that the human body is fragile.

Now, 45 years old I was back in a part of the sanctuary I hadn't seen since I was in my mid-teens. A quiet place of reflection and solitude, it had the same fireplace that was there in the early 1980s. A bit of a time-warp for me which I found comfort in as I settled into a chair.

The alter at Blessed Sacrament where I reflected on my life and prayed the day before my surgery. This photo was my screen saver on my phone while receiving treatment. I would think back to the day before my surgery and how cancer changed my life.

When the Sacrament is given, it is hoped that – be it God's will – I would be physically healed from illness. In a world of advancing science I also knew the skillful hands of surgeons and nurses would also be part of God's plan.

16

The spiritual side effect of the anointing is to be given courage and a gift of peace through my struggles. I am not saying I didn't curse God in anger during my fight. The times I did I tried to quickly turn my reflection back to the things that mattered. I learned quickly that self-pity is not attractive nor is it productive in your journey to get well. Maintaining your dignity is.

A Higher Power

Throughout my suffering I came to find that my soul would be uplifted through family and friends praying. Those friends who celebrated other faiths simply sent positive, or *"good energy"* my way.

The Catholic Church would say it was the Holy Spirit that I felt - the giver of life. It was this positive energy - a divine power - that continues to help me guide to others today in their times of darkness.

As you will learn later in the book, I believe my suffering and survival serves a purpose. The anointment was the beginning of another journey - a revelation to a different perspective on life, or perhaps simply it cleared my head to be aware of those around me who suffer.

Sucker Punched in the Breadbasket

The day before entering the ring for surgery I was sucker punched before I even entered the venue. I hope you never have to experience the *"how would YOU feel"* before cancer surgery. It is a feeling like no other; an emotional roller coaster ride. It was a restless, sleepless night.

Entering the Ring, the First Time

Feb. 8, 2012 ~ No Jokes this Morning

Scott is in surgery this morning. Please keep us in your thoughts and prayers today.

Check in at the hospital. At my request my mother took this photo as I waited to go to pre-op.

Round 1 – Surgery

I was at the hospital early the next morning. I went into pre-op, they gave me a gown and *"I love yous"* were said. Vitals were taken. No turning back… then I was put under.

Entering the Ring – Twice

I remember I awoke in a dark room feeling numb and fell back asleep. The next time I woke up in a panic *"I have to go to the bathroom!"*

"So go," said the nurse. Um, I forgot the urinary catheter was inserted during surgery, duh.

I was unaware of the amount of time I was in the operating room and later I found out that the tumor in the throat was deeper than the surgeon thought. I was in surgery several more hours than initially expected.

Feb. 8, 2012 – 4:12 p.m.

Scott is out of surgery and did great! The doctor said "the cancer is gone."

Round 2 – Pain Management

As the anesthetic wore off I was in pain. I was ordered morphine and as it was administered through the IV I could feel it go up my arm just like you see in the movies.

There was only one drawback: It didn't work. As it entered my core it didn't have any effect on my pain. I learned that day my body doesn't metabolize morphine well. Not a good time to learn that as you try to get your pain under control.

I remember my parents and wife coming in and out of the darkness to see me. It was a clouded evening. All I remember were bright hospital lights when moved to my hospital room.

Feb. 9, 2012 – 4:38 a.m.

Up all night. PAIN finally under control. Lots of downs, downs from one minute to the next.

It wasn't like anyone gave me a mirror after my surgery and said, *"look at your neck."* If they did I certainly have blocked that from my memory.

I know my parents and wife were literally shocked at the sight of the inflammation on my neck after the surgery as they would tell me later. The repression of the events doesn't bother me at all. I do feel sorry for my family as I know THEY do not have these memories repressed.

CORNERED

On Feb. 11, 2012, I took a post-op selfie of staples and an inflamed neck after seven cancerous Lymph nodes were removed. Drainage tubes in chest and a feeding (Nasogastric) tube inserted in a nostril to my stomach. After I took this photo I was in disbelief. I knew I had a long recovery ahead.

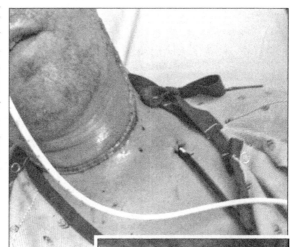

Feb. 15, 2012, shows the scar after staples were removed.

On Feb. 17, 2012, a mirror shows removed staples and a beat-down me. I cut shirts so I could put medicine on my scar.

On Feb. 18, 2012, I felt sorry for myself. Not flattering at all. I decided to put this photo in to encourage anyone who gets to this point.

Later in this book I talk about how cleansing crying is. Once you are done, move on.

19

Entering the Ring – Twice

Feb. 21, 2012, just a few days before I wrote "Sleigh Ride of Pain." The two "dot" scars on the left and right on my chest were from the drainage tubes that were removed.

On Feb. 22, 2012, I texted this photo to my wife, a thumbs up, I am sitting on the "Daddy" chair in the living room.

March 1, 2012, I just received news that the feeding tube would be removed. I haven't had a smile like this in a month.

As disgusting as it was, the feeding tube served its purpose and it was immediately trashed!

March 5, 2012, a happy Scott outside the Mayo Clinic.

Round 3 – Removal of Tubes

During surgery two drainage tubes were placed under my skin from my neck to upper chest. It's hard to explain but plastic suction devices were attached at the chest end to drain and flush out toxins. While in the hospital they were emptied by staff as they filled with blood, pus and other un-godly bodily fluids. One of the drainage tubes was removed before the other. In extreme pain, I screamed as it was pulled out. I had one more in and dreaded, DREADED, when the second would be removed. When it was finally pulled out I screamed. I'll never forget when I was told while still scream-ing that it was okay - that the second tube was removed and no longer in. Regardless I continued to scream. The pain was unbearable. As my pain subsided I released the tightness in my upper body and took a long breath.

Round 4 – You Have to Pee

It is not uncommon to have pain when a urinary catheter is removed from um, where it is removed from. Catheters are common during surgery and mine was no dif-ferent than any other. So when they remove it you take a deep breath and *"ouch-owee."* Simple, you're done, or so you think so.

I was told to go to the bathroom and pee. Once I did I would take a shower and be able to go home. Simple.

I stood in front of the toilet and started to go… *"stoppp!"* Pinch, pinch, I can't go it hurts to urinate. Stinging, burning, don't really know what to call it. *"Just keep try-ing"* I hear from the nurse in my hospital room.

I can't go so I go back to bed. I get up and try a few more times. *"Shit, really? This REALLY hurts."*

The nurse, *"Scott, if you don't start going to the bathroom we will have to put the catheter back in and you won't like that."* WHHHat? I'll be awake for that! I just re-ceived a low-blow right in the groin with no protective gear on.

I got up and out of bed again. Standing over the toilet, where I began to pee - stop, *"Our Father"* pee-pinch - stop, *"Who Art in Heaven."* Repeat again. *"Our Father"* pee-pinch - stop, *"Who Art in Heaven."* Repeating the Lord's Prayer got me through the pee-pain. What a story to tell, huh?

Feb. 13, 2012, 3:22 p.m.

Checking out from "Club Mayo"

I was admitted into the hospital on February 8 and discharged on February 13. My memory of the events at the hospital, time of day, who visited and when still remains cloudy in my mind to this day.

Final Bell Sounds, First Fight Over

My cancer was removed. I was told it was deeper in my throat than expected. I was blessed as some people come out of surgery with a tracheotomy and others have part of their tongue removed. It was a short fight.

A few days in the hospital but I had a tight recovery time before my next fight. I knew I had to quickly recover from surgery and get strong again. I was under pressure.

That's how it was and to this day I felt cheated. I was feeling so good by the end of March; I rolled with the punches and came out clean. In a few weeks another fight was scheduled, and this one would be an adjunctive therapy title fight. I was to dodge even more punches during chemotherapy and radiation treatments.

Fight Aftermath

Staples, Yea We Got That

Anne counted 48 staples removed from my neck mid-February. The scar runs from one ear down and across my neck to the other ear. I was asked if I wanted to keep the staples. I declined as each one hit the trash can when removed.

Feeding Tubes

Don't get into a bar fight and get your jaw wired shut. Don't get throat cancer. Both will require a short-term feeding tube.

There are two types of feeding tubes. After my experience and what I have heard of the abdomen (Gastrostomy) tubes, I feel lucky that mine was placed through the nose. With both types, you feed yourself with a high-protein drink through a port by attaching a large syringe to it. In the photo of me crying on page 19 you can see the port taped to my chest.

When feeding myself I quickly learned that my body had an intolerance to the high-protein drink as I had cold sweats and then my skin became clammy. At first we tried to water the supplement down but I felt bloated and couldn't finish the feedings.

I switched to a protein drink with fewer calories and was able to handle the feedings. This was at a cost, of course, as my calorie intake declined.

When my feeding tube was removed on March 1, I only had a few weeks to eat and gain weight that I lost.

Thinking about the removal today still gives me chills of excitement. I was done with an unnatural and evasive tube that was down my throat. The photos on page 20 truly tell the story of my elation that day.

22

CORNERED

I was told by my surgeon, *"Don't pass up a fast food drive-through."* I ate a lot of burgers and drank as many shakes as I could. At first I ate soft foods like the meal I got at Boston Market on March 2, 2012.

March 6, 2012

I stopped by Blessed Sacrament after treatment at the Mayo Scottsdale location on March 6, 2012. My Facebook post says it all.

"So I got me a pen and a paper and made up my own little sign. I said thank you Lord for thinking about me I AM ALIVE and doing fine." Since feeding tube has been out I've been feeling better. Got to work on calories and protein intake, but when you can only swallow puddings and creamed soup kinda makes it tough. I've been driving to my appointments which are many.

March 7, 2012

Appointment after appointment this week. Scary part is I've lost 20 lbs. and haven't started Chemo. Went to a nutrition expert yesterday. She wants 2200 calories in me and I am barely making 1600, with soups etc. She gave me an old recipe I used in college to gain weight with whole and dry milk. I'll be supplementing diet with that.

Fight Preparations

During this recovery time, I was taught neck, jaw and tongue exercises, and had gastroenterology office visits to check on my weight.

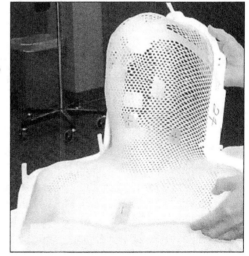

Other preparations included the making of custom mouth guards to be used during my radiation treatment. A special *"screen"* mask was custom formed to my face. This would be used to bolt my head to a table during radiation.

Ding, Ding Second Fight

I hadn't quite gained all of my strength back from surgery and here I was against the ropes once again. Each day – five days a week – I went to radiation treatment; once a week on Tuesdays I went to receive chemotherapy.

Entering the Ring – Twice

The experience began with *"I am past my first week"* to the countdown of the days left counting the rounds. I remember halfway through treatment wondering how I was going to continue on as the life was sucked out of me. I would wake up each day and look in the mirror and say, *"you can do this."* Even if I didn't think so, it would be said. This had become my mantra.

By the end of the adjuvant therapy I was exhausted physically, mentally, and spiritually brought to tears.

Six Rounds with Chemo
Stickin' it to the Man

I was told before surgery I may not have to have chemotherapy. I was advised afterwards that chemo would be a part of my adjuvant therapy due to how deep the cancer was in the back of my throat.

March 27 began my journey to the Ambulatory Infusion Center of the main Mayo hospital. Chemo was a tiring process: I was in at 7:45 a.m. and out at 6:15 p.m. This would be my routine for the next six Tuesdays to come.

I have heard horror stories of chemotherapy and the body's reaction to killing bad and GOOD cells. My experience was not horrific as some people have but my experience was surreal nonetheless. I was told I had a low dose of CISplatin and I cannot even fathom what a high dose would do to the body.

It was always easy for nurses to draw blood from my veins before cancer. Venipuncture as it is known was performed numerous times before my adjuvant therapy.

During the chemo treatment, just the thought of needles became so unbearable that I joked I was a human pincushion. Every Tuesday I would dread *"threading the needle"* because a vein would be missed. Most often nurses missed two, and in some weeks, three times. Each week a new nurse that was supposed to be the best of the best would miss her mark. It wasn't really their fault as I saw my veins getting thinner from treatment - towards the end it was tough to find a good vein.

I was never apprehensive about needles, but now I have to look away anytime blood is drawn. It takes me back to the exact moment of *"oh crap"* will they miss? That would begin my Tuesday morning.

CORNERED

At one of the treatments I had infiltration, where some of the fluid infused into the surrounding tissue in my forearm. It was painful and applying heat helped me get through that afternoon.

Oh and when the nurse puts on the protective gear to administer your treatment, you will feel like a radioactive nuclear reactor. It is okay for you to receive it, but the nurse takes every precautionary measure to protect herself. The biohazard symbol on the chemotherapy bag says it all.

The infusion center is cold and they provide you with warm blankets. Before chemo being cold didn't bother me. I actually had a tolerance for cold. Today a cold chill takes me back immediately to the center.

My experience could have been different. Some people have a port inserted into their upper chest to receive treatment. It's there as long as the treatment lasts.

I drove back and forth to the clinic until one day, towards the end of my treatment my throat was so sore from radiation that I asked for some pain meds. The IV was already in so the medicine could be administered quickly. That was the only afternoon that my mother drove me home. I pushed through each day and was proud that I was able to make it to the hospital myself. This was before Uber and Lift.

During this time I didn't post much to my blog. I had told people if I didn't post it was because I was going through a rough time. Chemo on Tuesdays would put me down until late Friday night. Tuesdays and Wednesdays would be the worst. I felt like cracked eggshells and didn't want to be touched. Physical contact made my body feel worse.

I would curl up in the fetal position and didn't want to eat or drink. I had sensitivity to light. I hated light. I'd say the last three weeks of my treatment I was in a haze with the fog around me darkening. Fatigue and tiredness followed, and at the same time hospital staff kept telling me to exercise so the endorphins would kick in to help me feel better. I had no such energy to do so.

Somehow I would still get up after chemo Tuesday and make it to my radiation appointments Wednesday through Friday after which I immediately returned home to rest and sleep.

(Right) At chemo treatment my neck still swollen from my surgery on April 3, 2012.

29 Rounds with Radiation

My radiation began on March 29 and ended May 8. Mayo staff would play music during the radiation treatment and they only had a few CDs. To this day I cannot listen to Nora Jones's first album as it reminds me of my head being bolted down.

If you receive this treatment you should practice taking yourself to your *"happy"* place before you are at the hospital. Seriously, you have to prepare yourself for this mentally as well as prepare yourself physically for chemotherapy.

If you are claustrophobic you will HATE radiation treatments. For 15 to 20 minutes you are lying down, with a mouth guard in to protect your teeth and your facemask is bolted down.

(Above Right) Visionalizing my opponent during radiation treatment.

(Right) I gave a thumbs up as my head was bolted down at my last radiation treatment.

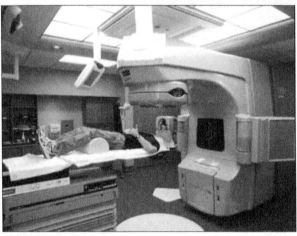

I used meditation techniques I learned at high school church retreats to rid my mind of any apprehension. I have a bad gag reflex and was worried early on that I would begin choking during treatment.

I did well until about two weeks before the end of my treatments. I started to gag and waved frantically so I could be unbolted from the table to remove my mouth guards.

It only happened once and that was enough for me. The next day I went into the zone as I lay on the table.

CORNERED

Your body will react to this treatment with dry *"cotton"* mouth and burned skin. Toward the end of treatment I could no longer swallow.

The pain goes beyond having tonsillitis or having strep throat. I was prescribed something called miracle mouthwash to gargle and numb the back of my throat.

(Below and right) Toward the end of my radiation treatments on May 1, 2012 with burns on my neck. Notice the weight loss.

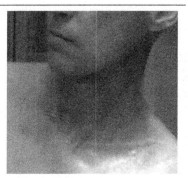

Keeping it Real

If you are an extrovert, get to know the staff where you are being treated. If you are not an extrovert, become one. I only say this as it will remind you of the *"real"* world that is outside as you continue on your quest to get well. You learn about quirky husbands or wives and what their children are doing, what funny thing their pet did the past week. Keeping it real will help you keep your sanity when you are inside of a treatment room every day.

My Caregiver and Friend

(Right) My spouse Anne and I on my last day of radiation treatment. She took care of our child, dog, house, you name it – she took care of me. I was told after, "you can't get sick again!"

I hope you have a caregiver (family member or friend) to support you. My wife Anne often talks about the frustration she had like me not drinking enough water or not *"eating"* enough of my protein drinks when using the feeding tube.

27

Entering the Ring – Twice

She would check on me, I'd say *"I will drink some water"* and an hour later she would find I had not touched the cup. For me, time stood still, for her it was an hour later.

She took care of our daughter during this turbulent time. Luckily my daughter was small enough that she doesn't remember a lot of Daddy's fight.

In May of 2012, I felt I was robbed of six months of my life and had missed experiences with my wife and daughter. I missed the Arizona Centennial celebration that I worked on a committee for several years because I was still in the hospital. I missed holiday gatherings, birthdays, and play time - all were lost. It wasn't until a few months later I realized that I was alive to experience all that life had to offer in my future.

Last Treatment ~ Two Anniversaries

As the weeks pass with treatment you do not want to do anything. No television watching; no book reading; forget about talking to friends or being social – priority one was winning the bout but I kept getting body punched and was out of wind.

Toward the end of treatment I was out of gas. I couldn't get angry anymore, I couldn't cry anymore. Stick a fork in me – I was WELL DONE and my neck and throat were fried. My body was broken down. I had lost more than 25 pounds. Weigh-ins would scare me because I was told if I didn't at least maintain my current weight, a feeding tube would be put into my stomach. I was trying to avoid that as much as possible.

In my last week of radiation others told me that there may be a feeling of being *"let down"* after you leave on your last treatment day. *"You may feel like coming back to visit,"* said one of the Mayo staff. For some, the home away from home has a lasting effect on one's psyche. They feel the need to be in their comfort zone.

My wife Anne came with me on my last day of treatment - May 8. It was to be a celebration of victory I will never forget. I must be honest. On that last day of treatment I had no such feeling to return. It was like my last day of college. It was time to move on.

"So you want your mask?" I was asked. I guess some people put decorative tile on it and hang it on the wall. Some people put their mask in the garden and make *"chia pets"* out of them.

I looked to my wife and said if I take it I would enjoy bringing it to the desert and destroying it with a shotgun. There was too much negative energy associated with that mask, so it was left behind with the emotional memories of having my head locked down on a table unable to move.

I rang a bell after my final treatment. My wife said I had tears in my eyes when I rang the bell. Photos were taken of me and staff as if they were high school friends on graduation day.

It seems so long ago now. I always need to be reminded of this day because of the feeling of pure joy. I was triumphant!

CORNERED

I am also reminded of this day because it is also my wedding anniversary. Anne and I celebrated our anniversary that day with lunch. I tried to eat chicken soup.

(Below) After my last radiation appointment, I rang a bell signifying the end of treatment. My hair thinned out and I lost hair on the back of my head. I had such high expectations that everything would change. Only you are the one who changes during the experience. The world remains the same. Sad but true.

My Best Friend Loses Her Fight

My last treatment was yet to be a few weeks old when my heart was ripped wide open. I couldn't believe it when it happened. The timing was way off and to this day I still don't understand why I lost my best friend after 13 years.

My black Lab girl, Shadow, started to act strange and was having seizures. During the dog's first seizure I freaked as my wife and daughter were out of the house on a Saturday night. I thought the dog was choking on something and I rushed her to the emergency animal hospital up the street.

She began to have accidents in the house and hide her head in corners. We had noticed a quick decline in her energy level and wondered why she lost her excitement to play ball.

We took her to our vet and then a specialist who confirmed that she had brain cancer. Hadn't my wife and daughter already endured enough pain with me being sick? Here was yet another low blow…I was devastated.

Entering the Ring – Twice

I was weak from my treatment and could barely walk myself. I'll always remember carrying Shadow into the vet wrapped in a blanket. I had no strength to carry her but the dog couldn't walk. I'll always remember her taking her last breath, and how I cried for 15 minutes next to her as she passed. It was a dark day after a dark six months.

Today I have two wonderful dogs but when I think back to May 19, 2012, and losing my *"first little girl"* my heart still aches.

May 16, 2012

Anne and I are heartbroken. Today I took our 13 year old Black Lab to a specialist for seizures she started having three weeks ago. We thought meds were not working right. She has been diagnosed with a brain tumor.

We are shocked and saddened. Just four weeks ago she was counter grazing stealing food, going on walks and full of life. Now she can barely stand.

Not now God, I don't want to lose my best friend and little terror.

Memorial Day Beer

It really is the simple things in life that you will miss during treatment. When I had the feeding tube, I posted that I missed drinking water and eating pizza the most. Water, yes and to this day every time I sip it, I swallow it without pain and remember that I missed drinking water.

On May 28, Memorial Day, I shared a post on Facebook of me drinking my first beer since December 26, 2011, the day I started to take my meds to control pain from my cancer.

"Can't taste it because of radiation treatments but I can feel the bubbles as I sip it." It was a Guinness. *"No light beer for me. Got to gain weight. Maybe this week will be my first coffee since before my surgery February 7."*

This was the beginning, a rebirth, of me trying new foods and drinks as my taste buds were changed forever after radiation.

Looking ahead – A Third Fight?

I hoped and prayed that this would be the last of surgeries and treatment as the ring of the final bell was certainly NOT a letdown.

During one of my visits Dr. Hinni said *"you should take a vacation when it is all over – to the mountains, to the beach – whatever you enjoy."* Anne loved that suggestion and made preparations to visit the beach at Coronado Island.

I was still weak when we went but enjoyed being the Daddy sherpa and attempting to carry my daughter on my shoulders.

CORNERED

By the end of May I had cabin fever and would be back to work in June. Looking back at that decision I would have taken another few weeks off as I was drained each day at work.

Really loved?

June 14, 2012

"Thank you co-workers," was my tweet and link to my blog which read, "Really loved? Or tired of delegated work? Yesterday was my first day back to work and I was greeted with open arms.

My office floor was covered with Sedona red Diamondbacks balloons that everyone wrote sayings on and signed.

Cancer free – Summer Results

So when are you truly *"cancer free?"* What day, if any, do you celebrate your "new normal?"

Aug. 9, 2012

At the Mayo Clinic

What? MORE blood drawn? Mayo vampires are sucking me dry this year. Hope to receive PET scan results today. Clear or not clear of all cancer? My bet is clear. Should know by 2:30 AZ time.

What kind of good news did you receive today? PET scan shows I am cancer free!

I keep two days close in my heart as anniversary dates. The *"eighths"* are remembered for the beginning and the end – February 8 and May 8.

Some survivors are scared for what the future may bring. Will the cancer come back? What would I do?

I haven't taken that approach to life. I cannot prevent something that may or may not come back. It is in God's hands. In the meantime I have a life to live with my wife, daughter, family and friends.

CHAPTER 6.

Who is Holding the Reigns?

Feb. 24, 2012

 The latest ramblings of a mind gone mad.

Sleigh Ride of Pain

It was right off the midway, was a small little ride, would have lost it in a blink of an eye;

The sign "Sleigh Ride of Pain" with an old man with a reign, sat in front of a sleigh asking, "why?"

The winds kicked up, my swagger was bold, didn't want to look back on my life;

A haggard face grinning, he said, "it's beginnin' you're ready to go under the knife."

The man then scanned, my one-way ticket in hand, with one crack of a whip I did ride.

I looked to his chair, the man no longer there; a demon would be by my side.

But the "Sleigh Ride of Pain" descends all earthly pains; because the demon let go of the reigns; spiral your way down, minutes tick into hours, the darkness consumes all your power.

I laughed when they said "how low can you go?" for fears are merely in mind;

"How low? I'll dig deep, find my inner most peace" the pain I would leave far behind.

But when awoke, a grim tale I was living; I found the hell too tough to swallow.

Who is Holding the Reigns?

Like a hound dog skunked I yelped with tail between legs, the shadows of darkness did follow.

But the "Sleigh Ride of Pain" descends all earthly pains; because the demon let go of the reigns; spiral your way down, minutes tick into hours, the darkness consumes all your power.

Demons of bone and demons of flesh and those who dance by the fire; the pains from the demons hear begging men screaming for the ride of your life to expire.

Lower yourself to the depths of your soul, and when you can go no lower; a fallen angel will say there is bedrock ahead it's got to begin to go slower.

It will never be low enough so it's been said, so listen to my tale of dread; for the sleigh ride's about to get faster, below bedrock you'll past her, still deeper you'll go in your head.

But the "Sleigh Ride of Pain" descends all earthly pains; because the demon let go of the reigns; spiral your way down, minutes tick into hours, the darkness consumes all your power.

Be prepared to be scared of the old man with the reign, in the front of the sleigh by the sign. Think twice about ridin' even though you're survivin' thoughts of pain soon to know will be gone.

CHAPTER 7.
Surviving Skills 101

As a survivor, I have found I am more aware of those around me who are suffering. These people are not only survivors of cancer or other medical treatments but survivors of war and other heart-breaking life experiences.

I have been at the *"right place at the right time"* to talk to these people. The odds of me being at that place have been surreal to me. It is usually a last minute choice in a direction change that brings me to someone in need. Call it fate, destiny, or kismet; I am here for a reason.

It is because of them that I have decided to pen my thoughts that I have shared with them. I am constantly amazed by the strength of the human spirit. People have said I am their inspiration, when in actuality they have provided me strength to aspire to be a better human being.

You can make a conscious choice about how you are going to react to a tragic or life-changing event. If you want to be cynical don't get cancer. You're in constant motion; you need to believe in yourself and your self-worth.

This chapter is filled with discussions that I have had with others since surviving. The *"survival skills"* listed in this chapter have brought me through some of my darkest hours. I have shared them with others and would like to share them with you.

Game Face On

I got some advice from one of my friends, Don Watters, who had cancer in his 20s - give your family and friends the *"game face."*

Sometimes people just do not know what to say or do, so make them feel at ease with the game face, even if you are at a low point.

Looking back I know my wife saw through the game face. Just remember to smile. When you go into the ring give yourself the game face, it's time, *"game on!"* time to take on each day as it comes.

Oh, and don't give the game face to your doctors, nurses and those treating you. They are trained to know what to say. They are there for you. And as they get to know you, they can see right through your game face. Even the woman who works the front desk knows your good from bad days! Smile as you walk in to your treatments.

The Stare-Down

You have no other choice. Well you do, but the alternative is doing nothing. Don't show up. Don't enter the ring. Don't stare down your opponent. Don't look cancer straight in the face. I would rather die trying than not know I didn't do everything I could to survive.

I found it difficult to hear after my surgery and during my treatment that people didn't do what the doctors told them to do.

I thought, *what?* Yes people decide to skip chemo and radiation treatments. They decide to stop taking medication. They decide when they had enough because their brain shuts down. You chose your coaching staff for a reason. Listen to them. They won't throw in the towel and stop the fight, you shouldn't either.

You're in a fight or flight situation and as long as you are breathing do what the doctors tell you. You have so much to live for and there are people on this earth that appreciate you.

Every morning since my diagnosis I say at least five times, *"I am going to be okay, I have no other choice."* I still say this every day even in year five when I am tired and have to push through each day.

Put Up Your Dukes and Fight

This is your fight. It is okay to ask for help but ultimately it is your fight to win. The saying is *"no one fights alone."*

You are the boxer in the ring. No one else is there. You have a trainer, a nutritionist, a cut man, and a corner coach and many more on your coaching staff. But when you are in the ring, it is your fight.

You'll look around and say *"hey, come on people help me."* Family and friends may not be able to help. They might not know how to help or support you. The doctors and nurses know how. Remember they are right over the ropes and in your corner.

During this experience I found that I understated my pain threshold. Instead of asking for help with the pain I fought through it. I didn't realize that my #5 on the pain scale was actually a #9. I realized that fighting didn't mean you had to suffer.

Each day my *"job"* was to fight – push through it, no backing down. Toward the end of the bout I was in a haze and all I could hear was the timer. Minutes, then to seconds of pushing through the pain and suffering. Literally, SECONDS… tick, tick, tick. I was in slow motion waiting for the round to end. After chemo I curled up into a ball. Every part of my body felt like it was going to just crack into little pieces.

Simply stated it is your fight. You have to take one round at a time. Some of the things that were easy when you were healthy become a battle -like going to the bathroom after the removal of a catheter.

Another reality check, and here it comes… you will lose some of the rounds. It's true. Fight until you have nothing left to give. Tomorrow is another day. If you fail, you fail. If you do loose the round from the previous day see the *"Cry"* and *"Get Angry"* sections of this chapter.

My battle cry was *"Don't let the bastard win."* What would yours be?

Cry

Before I was even diagnosed, I cried every day on the freeway to work as I struggled to get a biopsy on a lump on my neck. I cried looking into the mirror in disbelief. I cried going to appointments.

It's okay to cry. When you do, cry like you mean it. Let it out. It is cleansing.

The bathroom floor was my friend. I often would sit on it and cry when no one else was around; behind the door like a frightened child.

Pray

"There are no atheists in foxholes." As the saying goes in times of stress or fear, we find God or a higher power. Prayer can be meditative. Simply pray for strength to get through each day.

I would often visit the small chapel at the clinic after my treatments. Stopping in would depend on my strength, but I made it a point to visit whenever I could.

Since my experience, I have told doctors at the clinic and other survivors that during my treatment I would often find inner peace. And no, it wasn't when I was on medication.

Sometimes I would envision the alter photo on my phone in my brain and all was well. I struggle to this day to once again find this inner serenity as being back in the *"real"* world has stolen it from me.

Sounds strange, doesn't it? At least I felt the true presence of peace in some of my darkest hours.

Get Angry

If you get emotional and are all cried out, get angry. Yes it's okay to get angry. Anger is a human emotion and gets the adrenaline flowing.

Getting angry during your worst times will give you fuel to take on your next round. Simple challenges like getting out of bed, taking a shower or forcing myself to eat – I would use anger to get through even the simplest of tasks. I wasn't about to let the bastard win. Live with an angry vengeance.

Don't waste a great amount of time getting angry at God or a higher power. Although I felt close to God through prayer, I often cursed Him. Get angry at the cancer in your body, not God. When I got angry at God I quickly turned the anger toward the real offender, cancer.

It is only after you survive that you will understand there is a purpose to the madness although you may not know what it is quite yet.

Scream

Yes scream… this goes with getting angry. Sometimes you just have to let it out. Do it while no one else is around; you don't want to scare the crap out of your family. Sometimes my screams were a whimper as the radiation fried my throat, but I still let go a whimper.

How Low will You Go?

Sorry to say this, but someone has to tell you the truth. You will hit the canvas sometime in this experience. How you react after hitting it will make all the difference in your recovery.

(Left) You only have one choice. Yes, head and neck cancer will land more punches, but ultimately you will win the fight by KO.

At this point you will either be mentally or physically exhausted and you will have no stamina. Guess what? You'll go deeper into the abyss than you could ever imagine. It is a frightening thought but I've told people to expect a blow that will make you dizzy and disoriented. You will begin to doubt every punch you have thrown.

Your spirit will be tested. Your mind will tell you *"I can't do this"* but you can, you must, THERE IS NO OTHER CHOICE. This is where you have to dig deep into what your heart and soul is telling you.

When the fight is over and you finally climb out of the ring you'll find the sunrises much brighter and the sunsets more colorful. Your senses will be heightened.

CHAPTER 8.

A Fresh Start - After Winning the Fight

After becoming a survivor, I immediately wanted to focus on a fresh start. Once I gained some strength back I thought life would really be different. My mindset was to MAKE things different. As I have come to find in the last five years of survival, sometimes I only take one step forward and two steps back. I fight daily for balance but still appreciate the smallest of things.

New Normal

This is a catch-phrase term that everyone uses with survivors. I have a problem with it because nothing in life is normal. It is constantly changing and evolving. Hopefully, you learn from your mistakes, revel in your accomplishments and always move forward, whether you're a cancer survivor or not.

Secondly, I don't think I've ever been normal. Just ask my family and friends. Life is a journey with ebbs and flows and each journey is unique unto itself. Why not be like I've been from the start, abnormal? Take it from there and just when you think you've found a *"new"* normal, the normal changes. It's called life. No journey is perfect.

Defining Life's Experiences

Since my experience, my wife has continually said don't let *"it"* define you. Yes I have said already there has been a transformation within me and I do feel a sense of purpose. It's not like I live every day jumping in the streets saying, *"Hey look at me, I am a cancer survivor! Woo-hoo! I deserve to be treated differently."*

Without getting too philosophical your life is defined by how you REACT to experiences. How did you react to that left hook? Sometimes you get nailed by one even when your guard is up. There will never be a good time to get cancer. There will never be a good time for... you fill in the blank.

When you take your last breath what have you learned? Did you share your knowledge with others to give them hope? Surviving is a life-changing experience I'll never forget.

A Fresh Start - After Winning the Fight

I only look back to remind me of my successes and to motivate me to get my ass moving. Some of the photos in this book are shocking and disturbing to look at. I draw strength from them.

I have been telling others don't look back and wonder what if? What if I had done this or that? What a waste of time. If you did that before your surgery and treatment I suggest you stop. Stop right now!

Looking back on any experience is hard to do but it does serve a purpose. Don't dwell on the *"it."* Celebrate that you made it through your nightmare. You had setbacks, highs and lows and a lot of self-doubt. You succeeded by pushing forward.

I believe cancer survivors have a unique life story. Stories that I hope you will have the courage to share. I challenge you to share your story.

You will probably never move past *what* happened. You should stop asking *"why me?"* The why it happened will never be answered. The reason it happened is a different story.

Be God-like, not God

I have met a few cancer survivors who are arrogant - they beat the odds and feel like the world owes them. Wow! I don't know what they experienced in their darkest hours. They continue to live their life without purpose and believe only in themselves.

They look at their life-changing experience as if they were the Almighty himself and the gift of life was theirs for the taking. This personality trait was theirs long before they were diagnosed. What a sad state to be in.

(Right) Out of my darkest hours CopperState Survivors, a cancer running support group was formed.

How can I forget being told; on January 2 - at the beginning of the New Year - I have cancer? Perhaps it happened this way to remind me that life is more than 365 days around the sun. Every day on this earth should be celebrated. Some days of celebration are easier than others but you should thank a higher power you are still here.

CORNERED

Purpose

If you hit the canvass, gotten up, hit the canvass again, and climbed out of the ring and are breathing you have probably already thought about your purpose. You are here for a reason. You're alive and you're awake. If you've gotten past what has happened and have gained some strength back now, you have a choice to live with a purpose. I don't mean to be obtuse or belittle you if you choose not to live with a new purpose. If this is the case, I hope you live to inspire. Live a life you've always wanted to live not the way you think others want you to live. Look at each day as if it were your last on this earth. Learn to trust your instincts and yourself.

Perhaps you will choose to keep your story to yourself. If you do, I hope you still marvel at the gifts in life. A simple smile on your face every day will make others envious.

During treatment I dug deeper into my self-worth and never surrendered. Surviving cancer has cleared my vision. It has strengthened me. It hasn't increased my feelings of self-worth but it has increased my ability to RECOGNIZE my self-worth.

I Can't Complain About my Cancer

Sure I could, but why? People ask, *"How are you doing today?"* Some know about my journey, others do not. I simply say I am having a great day. With those that I have shared the journey I say, *"I am having a great day. And even if I am not, it's better than the alternative."* At the end of two years in remission people stopped asking how I was feeling. Healing takes time and the daily struggles continue to be real.

The Cancer Card

Around my third year, if I mentioned my struggles or talked about scars that won't heal, I was told by some that I was *"pulling the cancer card."* I wasn't complaining I was simply explaining why I did certain things, like gagging when eating.

Some people think you shouldn't have any issues because you are in remission. I am not saying I am owed anything because I survived, but I am owed some compassion as a human being.

Scars that Won't Heal

I still have daily struggles that I do not share with others. Other survivors will too. The effects of surgery, chemo and radiation are long-lasting.

Oral hygiene continues to be a priority as radiation gives you dry mouth. *"Really?"* Others will look at you with a strange curiosity. *"I hadn't thought of that."*

Dry-mouth, swallowing, chemo fog, fatigue and lack of energy, etc. you get my point. I still can't feel my neck from the scar to my Adam's apple. I'll never feel it. It is the reality of the situation.

A Fresh Start - After Winning the Fight

I immediately think about those who can't feel their arm or leg because they no longer *have* it. Maybe it's due to medical reasons, an accident or they served in the military and an IED took a limb. These are amazing people who are fighting bigger battles and challenges than I. Kind of puts my neck into perspective, now doesn't it?

Some people react to my trouble swallowing as a joke. Perhaps they do not know how to react because it makes them feel uncomfortable but it's a serious issue.

I have gotten food caught in the wrong *"pipe"* and a few times it has been scary. I went to the bathroom in 2015 and literally had to hack up some food to breathe. In early 2017 when I began to complete the edits of this book, a flat noodle was lodged in my throat and I coughed up so hard that I threw up on myself. I was on my way back to work from lunch.

What did I do? Cleaned myself up, went back to work and put on my running clothes. I finished out the day without any excuses. That would have been a good day to *"pull the cancer card."* But I am not that guy.

So what? I sometimes choke while eating. I am still eating, right? I continue to chew, chew, chew. Eating is now a chore. I was the first one done at the meal; now I am the last. I often give up trying to finish what's on my plate because of swallowing issues. There was a time when I enjoyed eating. Now I chose my meals with caution, and look to foods that go down easy. Do you choose the foods based on being worried you won't be able to swallow them?

And the swallowing problem gives way to the issue of maintaining my weight. I have always had a high metabolism and ate a lot to maintain weight before my cancer. As if maintaining weight is as much of a joke as gaining weight because of medications or surgery.

I shared with my radiologist that I am trying new foods, and revisiting the ones that I didn't like because radiation fried my taste buds. I am eating brussel sprouts now and my favorite beer has changed. I'll never forget the smile on his face when I told him that I am learning to taste again and find new foods to enjoy.

I am not sharing these stories for sympathy. I share them as fact. You have the choice on how to respond to the side effects that you cannot change.

I thank God for simple things that others take for granted. Being able to walk, being able to SEE another person smile. There are things to be grateful for even if YOUR scars, whether internal or external, won't heal. You just have to consciously be aware of them.

Survivor Encounters

In my fourth year of remission, someone used the term empath to describe me. I guess it is a common term but I had never heard it. It is simply the ability to read and feel another person's emotions.

CORNERED

As I said earlier in this book, the circumstances of meeting someone at the right time and place, which happens to me often now, is almost mystical to me. I was already outgoing before my surgery and would have probably struck up a conversation with these people anyway, but it wouldn't have been like it is today.

I want to share a few encounters that I've had since my cancer surgery.

I had just finished the D-Backs 5k Against Cancer. I decided to get some lunch in celebration of finishing the race and went to a downtown restaurant.

To my left was a veteran having a beer. He had recently returned from a deployment in Iraq. As with many soldiers returning from a war zone, he saw and heard things he will never tell his wife, closest family members or friends, but he shared them with me.

This survivor's world was falling apart. His wife was leaving him and family and friends didn't understand his pain. He shared horrors that only he knew: children with explosive backpacks, the difficulty of discerning who is friend or foe, coping with losing a brother-in-arms. Why did he share these dark secrets with me that day? I was there to listen and give a fellow human being compassion. He needed to know that his world would be okay and that it was okay to seek help.

I'll share another story; this one of a woman who was in the hallway with her husband as I was waiting to have a swallowing test in the fall of 2012. She had the same cancer as I and had a feeding tube in her nose. She was talking to her husband and was discouraged about her progress. After a discussion with her, I found she was maintaining her weight and her prognosis was good. She had surgery two weeks earlier. She looked at me in disbelief as I told her I wished I looked as good two weeks out of surgery. A smile and words of encouragement, that's all it takes from someone who is part of the *"club."*

Were these encounters by chance? I don't really know. I do know that I have had contact with many people who needed me to listen. I don't take on their burdens, I simply listen. I tell them of my own experience and it seems to add some perspective and ease their pain.

Chain Reactions and Triggers

Your brain and body are expected to react to your life experiences. As I stated earlier, I was never bothered by cold weather. Now, a cold chill takes me back to that moment when I was on the chemotherapy floor. Let that emotion end there. Don't go into the negative experience of being on the floor and what happened to you there. Immediately put on a jacket and some gloves and deal with it.

Some cancer survivors do not have visible scars; other scars are hidden. If you look in the mirror and see the scars it may take you back to some negative feelings. I have chosen to wear and show my scar as a badge of honor, one that shows survival is possible.

If triggers are pulling you down and you feel you cannot cope after surviving, get help. Don't wait. Your mental health should not be taken for granted just because family or friends say you should be okay. *"That was three years ago,"* someone once said to me. Like I was supposed to say, *"yea, you're right – it doesn't bother me. Thanks for the encouraging words."*

If you are turned away while trying to get help, go somewhere else. I have met some survivors who have hit rock bottom and don't have family or a support system in place. I talk to them to give them hope. You can make the difference.

The gift of surviving is understanding there are people on this planet who are going through trying times. They are sitting right across from you at a restaurant. That person crying? Sitting alone? Perhaps you are there at that moment to encourage them, to listen.

We live in a world of uncertainty. Some people who have the same treatment as I will lose their fight. I don't have survivor's guilt and I don't claim to have the answers as to why some people survive and others don't; no one knows. I only know I survived.

I have been blessed to still be here because of skilled surgeons, doctors and nurses. I have told them and my family and friends I believe a higher power has more for me to do.

I end with this quick story as I reflect on the reality of a man I saw during my treatment who is no longer with us.

During my chemo, each week, a man came in for his treatment and had been told he had one year to live. I remember how sad he was when he talked about his wife not yet having come to terms with him dying, but *he* had come to terms with it. He said he lived a full life.

He would come in happy to be alive, smile, and greet each person with a friendly *"hello."* He would ask how their day was going; he knew everyone's name. He was at peace.

What an inspiration. These types of people are all around you.

You need to be at peace with the cards that you have been dealt. I pray you find that peace and live a full life as well.

Epilogue

Feb. 8, 2017

At lunch

Five years ago today in the early morning I went into surgery to remove the cancer in my throat and neck.
The reflection in the mirror today still shows the scar and is a daily reminder of the battle. At five years, I continue to look at life through survivor glasses where your perspective is different. The sunrises are a little brighter now; the memories made are more heart felt because you live in the moment.

After the Facebook post on Wednesday, February 8, I had feeling in my neck – it was not a good feeling. I was in severe pain. I had an earache. The symptoms were all too similar to those described in this book in December of 2011. That Friday, I had made an appointment with my surgeon. Over the weekend I took ibuprofen to deaden the neck pain.

After an early Monday morning examination there was enough concern for me to get a CT scan which was scheduled much later in the day. I waited that afternoon in somewhat disbelief. I took this book to edit, and joked with the Mayo staff as I got the procedure done. It was a long week as I waited to get the test results the following Friday.

The main thing I want to tell you is that my doctors have told me I am healthy. My surgeon said it *"would take cosmic intervention"* for the cancer to come back. Good news. I am blessed. I don't know why I felt the pain but do know the experience heightened my senses once more and got me to again focus on my purpose.

This epilogue has been re-written many times since I started this book. Some were overly positive and some included negative energy. After writing a cancer survivor book why would I want to end it on a negative note? This is a question that I reflected

Epilogue

upon as I prepared to send it to print. Perhaps I was being pessimistic because I feel I should be physically stronger at year five. I certainly feel a lot better than I did after the first year of survival. But I am still tired, my energy level is low; I still struggle to maintain. Sometimes I just crash and have to sleep. I move slowly when I get out of bed in the morning. When I try taking time to rest my brain dwells on work at the office or my to-do list. I must admit I feel guilty because I have always tried to do my best and be there for everyone else.

My fatigue hasn't necessarily gotten worse; it just continues to be there. Like in other stages of my journey I am not going to hide how I feel in this book. After five years I am tired of being tired and I am tired of putting on the game face. I want to let other survivors know that being tired is just part of the deal. It is going to be okay. I have been told by other survivors my energy level will increase as time goes on. It is what it is.

If you are reading this book to support a loved one or friend who has been diagnosed with cancer, I ask that you also take time for yourself. I hope it gives you some insight to feelings they may not share with you. I do ask you to remember your loved one will continue to have fatigue years after treatment. They haven't changed and become lazy. They are not trying to purposely let you down if they don't accomplish something they said they would do. And they aren't making excuses, the fatigue is real.

I must admit to you that I have fallen back into the life *"trap"* something I thought I would never do after becoming a survivor. At least I still have my survivor glasses on that have transformed my perspective on life. I do have a problem with those who have the wrong prescription and look through their lenses with a distorted view of life. I am, as my surgeon noted after talking to him in year four, *"Tired of the bullshit."* When I feel like I've hit a wall I look at the photos in this book for inspiration and re-read my journey. It is still *my* choice on how I respond to the daily grind and the roadblocks of life. The journey has been challenging, and I must press on. But I guess we all get tired at a certain age. *"Don't get old,"* my grandmother used to say jokingly.

If you're a survivor or terminal I am not going to pretend to begin to know your feelings. This book is about my journey and my feelings. You have your own destiny to fulfill.

I do know a few things: You will always have purpose. You are here for a reason. I hope you choose to live your life to inspire. Don't give up.

I pray you find peace like the man I mentioned in my last chapter who came to terms with knowing he wasn't going to live much longer. You may be silent and I may not know you but you are *my* inspiration. Please remember you are not alone.

- Scott Cancelosi, March 3, 2017

About the Author

Scott Cancelosi (pronounced Cancel-oh-see) lives in Phoenix and had his cancer surgery and treatment at the Phoenix Mayo Clinic Campus.

Scott has a Bachelor's degree in journalism and public relations from Northern Arizona University, Flagstaff, Ariz. He has worked for the Arizona Secretary of State's office since 1996. Before beginning his career as a public servant, he worked in the newspaper industry and on business publications.

Scott has been labeled by his friends as a "mediocre" guitar player and singer-songwriter. His other hobbies include photography, downhill snow skiing and being the team captain for CopperState Survivors, Team CopperState an Arizona-based running group.

Scott lives in Phoenix with his wife Anne, daughter Maria, a Labrador retriever, Rocky and Australian Shepherd, Luna.

Also Available from This Author

Making the Days Count - My Countdown Cancer Journal
This journal is geared specifically toward cancer patients and their journey of counting
down the days to the end of treatment.

Available at
amazon

PROUDLY PRINTED
inTHE USA

25 Adventures & Things to Do, Before I Die
This book provides the framework to set a goal, accomplish it, and archive the experience for family and friends
to enjoy for years to come. It's all in one book. Your
bucket list, journal and photos.

Printed in Great Britain
by Amazon